SOME
CITY
GLASGOW

SOME CITY
GLASGOW
ROBIN WARD

Richard Drew Publishing Limited
1982

For My Parents

Richard Drew Publishing Limited
20 Park Circus, Glasgow G3 6BE
First Published 1982
Reprinted July 1982
© 1982 Robin Ward
ISBN 0 904002 88 8

Designed by Robin Ward
Photoset in Baskerville
Made and printed by Butler & Tanner Limited, Frome, Somerset

'What ever is good in its kind ought to be preserved in respect to antiquity,
as well as our present advantage, for destruction can be profitable to none
but such as live by it.'

Nicholas Hawksmoor, architect 1661-1736

The Christian Institute, Bothwell Street — demolished 1980

INTRODUCTION

This book is an evocation of Glasgow and its Victorian past with reference to the city's surviving 19th-century architecture. The drawings *do not* represent a complete survey of the city's older buildings, but they do illustrate the astonishing variety of Glasgow's Victorian architecture and the often improbable cross-cultural connections which contribute to its visual richness. There is a Venetian palace on Glasgow Green, there are Parisian and Egyptianesque tenements and commercial buildings, Grecian churches, Scottish Baronial style banks and, in the city's wind-swept hill-top cemetery, 19th-century tombs in every architectural style imaginable.

Much has been written of Glasgow's Victorian past and, to an extent, its architecture. But as we continue to undervalue and destroy our 19th-century heritage its quality and importance still need to be defended. Glasgow's post-war record on town planning and appreciation of its architectural heritage has not been good. The huge redevelopment schemes of the 1960s' obliterated many irreplaceable 19th-century buildings and the established communities of which they formed a part in pursuit of half-baked planning theories, political kudos and short-term economic greed.

You cannot entirely blame Glasgow for being seduced by the planners' vision of a modern city of Los Angeles freeways and space-age buildings. The same civic pride which built the glorious marble interiors of the Victorian City Chambers convinced those responsible that they were doing the right thing. Now these grand plans have been discredited. Glasgow's *futureworld* is a bleak failure. Utopia isn't created with the wreckers' ball.

Of course Glasgow, even in Victorian times, never was Utopia. Yet to many of its citizens it was, and still is, the next best thing. They have a passionate pride of place. Those who know the city only by its reputation for violence and so-called urban deprivation can never be aware of its noble architectural heritage and 19th-century prosperity.

Then, Glasgow was the second city of the British Empire, a vast smoky metropolis founded on the 18th-century American tobacco trade and 19th-century manufacturing — textiles, shipbuilding, steam locomotives, iron, coal and chemicals. Between 1870 and 1914 for example, Clyde shipyards alone produced 18 per cent of the world's steamships, and at their peak, just before the First World War, this was closer to one-third. By the 1890s Glasgow was building more steam locomotives than any other centre in Europe. A staggering 71 per cent were for export, mainly to the colonies.

Glasgow also had a flourishing turn-of-the-century cultural and artistic life of European stature surfing on the wave of the city's industrial success. Yet the city has none of the polished, civilised veneer of, say, Paris, Vienna or, for that matter, Edinburgh. Glasgow was primarily an industrial city. Its monuments to art, civilisation and the British Empire were never grand, planned imperial gestures like the 'Ringstrasse' in Vienna or the Parisian boulevards. Certainly the city has its share of ostentation – civic buildings like the City Chambers and the Art Galleries. It has genuine architectural masterpieces – Charles Rennie Mackintosh's Art School and 'Greek' Thomson's bizarre St Vincent Street Church. However, Glasgow's unique architectural heritage lies not so much in the isolated monuments as in the surviving examples of 19th-century commercial and industrial buildings, tenements and terraces. These seemingly commonplace Victorian buildings achieve a level of architectural distinction in Glasgow unequalled elsewhere in Britain. They form a Victorian townscape of incomparable concentration and variety – an architectural paradise. They represent the trade and industry on which the city grew and provide the historical context without which the palatial City Chambers and its like would become fossilised follies in an architectural desert.

These 19th-century buildings stand as reminders of the time when Glasgow was a great city. They hold poignant, perhaps often imagined, memories of better days. Much of the confusion and bewilderment which has afflicted Glasgow in the form of misguided planning policies of recent years has stemmed from an inability to come willingly to terms with the city's swift decline and to understand the singular circumstances of the time when it was the 'workshop of the British Empire'. Glasgow's politicians still speak with a Victorian breadth of confidence and ambition, but the industry and commerce to back them are long gone. Even shipbuilding, which for so long sustained the city's reputation, is now only a reflection of its former self. The majestic forest of cranes which once bestrode 20 miles of riverbank has been pulled away, leaving only solitary clumps of this ennobling activity. 'We don't just build ships here', a Govan shop steward once remarked, 'we build men'. Not anymore. And the decaying inner-city docks and silent wharves will never again witness fleets of steamships bound for Brisbane and Bombay, Cape Town and Calcutta, Singapore and Shanghai, Vancouver or Valparaiso.

These romantic destinations may have gone, but Glasgow still possesses the architecture of an empire, a Victorian legacy of rich splendour. It is an architecture marooned in time, yet it can still give pleasure and a continuity to our lives. Glasgow's future can never equal its past heyday – nothing can possibly restore the circumstances in which the city grew. The city's future pride must lie mainly in the conservation of its past and it is important that we have some regard for this instead of simply knocking it down.

There are encouraging signs in Europe and America of a changing attitude towards Victorian buildings. They are beginning to acquire a charisma of time and their architectural qualities, once scorned, are being reassessed. This new view of 19th-century architecture has not exactly taken Glasgow by storm, but it has had some effect. Demolition, once the easy option, is not as extensive as it was. Many 19th-century commercial buildings in the city centre have been stone-cleaned and renovated, and extensive restoration schemes for the city's surviving tenements have been carried out. But the bulldozers still lurk round the corner, engines running. Notable 19th-century buildings continue to fall victim to a combination of planning ineptitude and, with demolition for so long commonplace, local apathy and resignation.

Glasgow's history, particularly its Victorian history, is inspiring. The confidence and pride of those times linger on today, and this is a hopeful sign. The city and its people have a gritty dignity and resilience and much of the past survives. But without the magnificent 19th-century buildings to look at there can be neither inspiration nor hope. We can admire and value what remains of this heritage or we can ignore it. If we ignore it this splendid inheritance will vanish for ever and our lives, and the lives of those who follow us, will be diminished by its loss.

Glasgow does not present its beauty in an easily accessible way. It is not an obvious tourist attraction. It is a city of vivid visual contrasts – the pathetic world of urban decay lying just a stone's throw away from the ornate Victorian buildings in the city centre. It takes some effort to understand and appreciate this. The city is too easily dismissed as not being worth the bother. But ultimately it rewards those with the patience to get to know it and its people – those who take the time to walk its streets, stopping occasionally to look up at the wonderful façades above the shopfronts.

The city which the Victorians built in a hectic imperial Klondike from 1850 to 1914 was, architecturally, one of the finest of its era in Europe, if not the world. Despite two world wars, the unexpected but inevitable collapse of the Empire and the barbaric ravages of recent redevelopment, Glasgow remains today, in somewhat dilapidated splendour, a Victorian city *par excellence*. It is an architectural lost world still awaiting discovery as I hope the drawings in this book show.

Robin Ward 1982

14

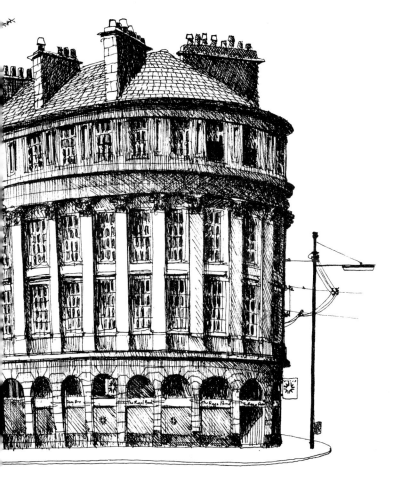

Glasgow is a city of tenements. Once scorned as dilapidated symbols of an older order, their architectural merits are now being appreciated. These buildings give Glasgow its unique architectural character. They stride up and down the city's hilly topography and line its streets in mesmerising half-mile long perspectives with a robust dignity characteristic of the Victorian age when they were built.

This range in Minerva Street (1853) is a fine example. Four storeys high with a well-proportioned façade topped by a pattern of chimney pots, it has the added grandeur of Corinthian pilasters and ground floor arches where the corner swings round into Argyle Street.

The last 20 years has seen widespread
demolition in Glasgow's tenement
areas. Whole communities have been
remorselessly obliterated. Street-
scapes of derelict tenements (shown
here in Springburn) have long been
commonplace. Fortunately, the
' bulldozer ' approach to town
planning has been discredited and
tenement restoration is now a
fashionable and economic alternative
to the wrecker's ball.

Glasgow, paradoxically and not
before time, is setting an example to
other cities, employing a less
destructive approach to urban

renewal by renovating many of its Victorian tenements. This 1890s' block in Woodlands Drive is one of many, in an award winning scheme, to have been recently restored.

Glasgow's tenement houses possess an architectural nobility which is absent in the mass-housing of other 19th-century cities. That many became slums was more a result of late 19th-century overpopulation and 20th-century planning mismanagement, rather than any fault of the architects.

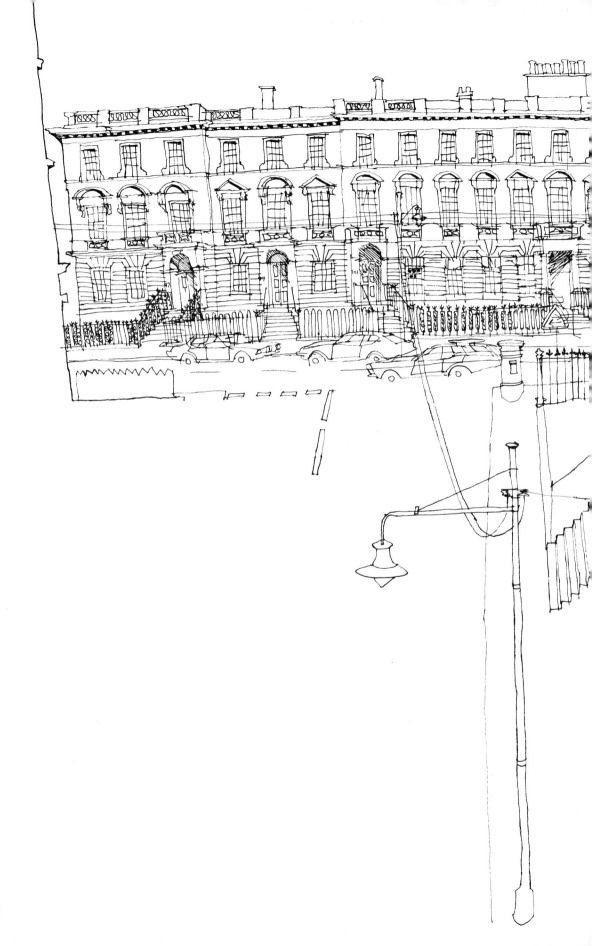

18

Most of Glasgow's surviving tenements were built in the industrial
boom years 1870 to 1910. Breadalbane
Terrace, perched on top of Hill Street,
is a rare (1845) example from earlier
days. Restoration seems to have
passed it by. It stands decaying and
forlorn, obviously having seen better
days.

Its design shows the influence of,
believe it or not, Italian Renaissance
palazzos, the proportions of which
Glasgow's Scottish tenement builders
happily adapted. Although no longer
exactly a palazzo, its porticos and
ornate cast-iron railings suggest it was
originally built for Glasgow's wealthy
businessmen. Aloof on its hill, it
certainly looks to have been dignified
enough for them.

This building, in Cowcaddens, is an unusual variation on the tenement theme. The front end is a branch of the Savings Bank, which explains the huge dome and decorated doorway – bankers have always had architectural pretentions. At the rear are several superior Victorian apartments with tiled closes and ornamental wooden banisters.

The building sits confidently on its triangular site – a busy tramway junction before the area was flattened by the urban motorway. Then the Savings Bank seemed to lean forward like a Clydebuilt ship, parting seas of traffic in New City Road. Today it stands in solitary grandeur, a beached liner on a deserted shore.

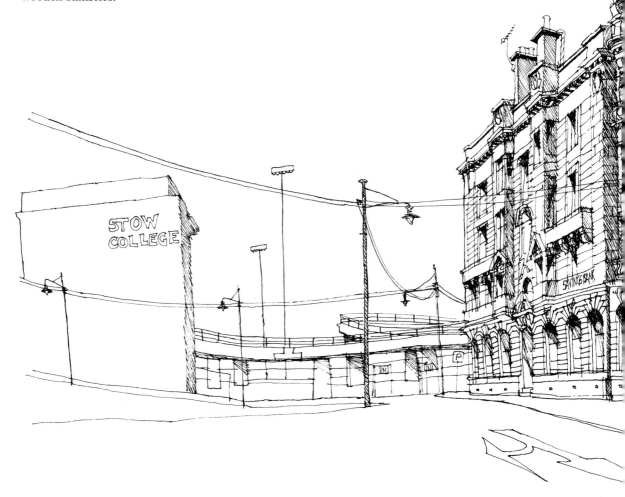

Disneyland in Broomhill? Well, not quite. Simply a Glasgow tenement designer's architectural flight of fancy. What hysterical dreams of baronial splendour he must have had to create such an absurd fancy! The Victorians' delight in decoration, a counter to the industrialisation of the time, knew no bounds. This architectural curio was taken quite seriously in 1902.

Glasgow's tenements often do appear wearing some sort of architectural disguise: Greek, Egyptian, French Second Empire; but none quite achieve the gloriously ridiculous effect of Inverclyde Gardens.

This building is the ultimate in Glasgow tenement design – an elaborate 1891 apartment block sweeping majestically into Sauchiehall Street with an architectural panache typical of its time.

Charing Cross Mansions was designed by Sir J. J. Burnet, one of Glasgow's most eminent Victorian architects. It looks remarkably like a scaled-down version of the Hotel de Ville in Paris which the architect must have seen while studying in that city. Above the rippling sandstone of the curved façade are romantic skyline details clearly showing the Parisian influence which inspired this wonderful building.

In the left foreground is the terracotta Cameron Fountain. Made by the Doulton Company in 1896, its French Renaissance style adds a further Gallic touch to the Charing Cross area. Glasgow's finest fountain however is the incomparable 1888 Victoria Fountain on Glasgow Green (also Doulton terracotta). It is, unfortunately, badly vandalised and in need of repair.

West of Charing Cross is another Glasgow architectural landmark – the skyline towers of Free Church College (1856/61) and Park Church (1856/57). They rise above the early Victorian terraces of Woodlands Hill like churches of a lost Italian hill town shivering, rather than shimmering, in Scotland's less sunny northern climes. The Italianate style of Free Church College heightens this impression, and these dramatic towers punctuate an area whose noble streets are among the finest examples of Victorian town planning in Europe.

A much older city tower is the steeple
of St Andrew's Church (1739/56)
tucked away near Glasgow Cross in
the old merchants' area. The city's
18th-century tobacco lords used to
praise the Lord for their profits here
before the city's commercial and
residential areas drifted westwards,
leaving St Andrew's a forgotten
building.

   Its design was based on St Martin's-
in-the-Fields, London, although the
steeple is more Baltic, rather than
classical, in inspiration. You expect
Hamlet to speak from the bell tower.
Inside there is a riot of Rococo
plasterwork of outstanding quality.

The oldest church building in the city is Glasgow Cathedral. It is not a large Gothic church compared with its contemporaries elsewhere in Europe and is best seen from the south east where rising ground heightens its presence. It then begins to command the area around it as a great cathedral should.

Construction began in the late 12th-century and although added to over the years (the steeple is 15th-century) it has retained a visual balance and sober, if solemn, dignity.

Two ungainly towers were removed by the Victorians who planned an excessive scheme to ' improve ' the west front with two ponderous Gothic Revival towers. Fortunately this ill-advised plan was never carried out. The Victorians built splendid new buildings, but their modifications of older structures were less successful.

29

Glasgow is graced by a marvellous collection of church towers and steeples. These once jostled for attention among now long demolished factory chimneys. Today they are beacons of faith and humanity amongst the high-rise flats.

Many of these churches were built in Gothic style – traditional for religious buildings in Northern Europe. Other styles were employed, particularly Greek – different religious denominations had their favourite types of architecture. But in 19th-century Glasgow, Gothic was the most popular.

The example shown here, once Partick Newton Place Church, is fairly typical of the style and quality of these buildings in the city.

St Jude's Free Presbyterian Church, built in 1874/76 is another fine example of ecclesiastical Victorian Gothic in Glasgow. The architectural origin here is France. The building has a graceful steeple of eloquent proportions and the belfry is decorated with groups of saintly stone figures. A closer look reveals some ferocious imaginary beasts clinging to the walls – pagan

spirits about to pounce on unwary
members of the congregation, or
perhaps those over-tempted by the
off-licence across the road.

The congregation of Cunninghame Free Church in Ballater Street have little to be thankful for. The tenement community which existed in this area has been scattered by comprehensive re-development leaving this abandoned church standing in a barren wasteland. Familiar surroundings and buildings have been wiped off the map. This beautiful little church too, has since been pulled down.

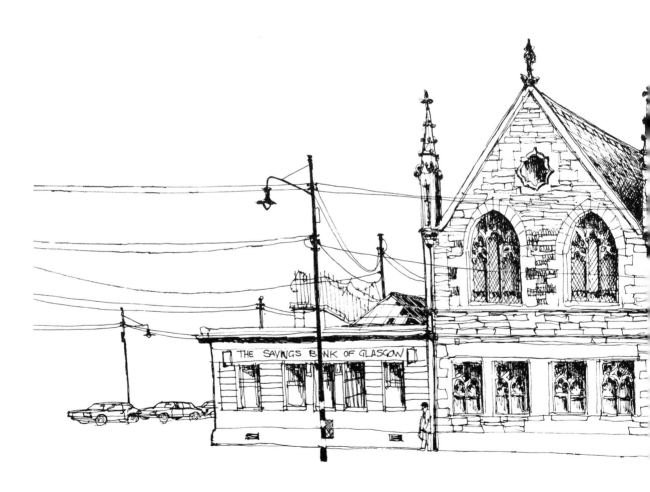

This is St Vincent Street Church (1857/59), designed by Glasgow's most original and talented architect of the mid-Victorian period. Alexander ' Greek ' Thomson. Thomson never travelled far, but he was undoubtedly influenced by books on Greek architecture and Victorian travellers' tales of the empire and by the contemporary interest in the antiquities of Greece and Egypt.

The Victorians, unsure of their cultural identity in a time of industrial change, looked to the past for aesthetic advice. They freely used any obsolete architectural style they thought would confer a surface of good taste and dignity on their buildings and themselves. This practice resulted in the amazing profusion of styles which a Victorian city like Glasgow exhibits.

Few architects could do anything other than imitate the glory of Greece, Rome, or Egypt. But Thomson could interpret a worn-out style in an original way, as St Vincent Street Church demonstrates.

The building occupies a steeply sloping site which allowed Thomson to manipulate the basically Greek design in a breathtaking series of plinths and pediments which culminate in the splendidly bizarre Indian/Egyptianesque tower. It looks as if it was built for some Moghul potentate rather than the United Presbyterian Church. This unique building is one of the architectural masterpieces of 19th-century Europe. The modern block behind, although of some distinction, is eclipsed by comparison.

Apart from churches, Greek-style
villas, terraces, and tenements,
Thomson did a nice line in
warehouses. Buildings such as the
Grecian Building (1865) in
Sauchiehall Street show his obsessive
pursuit of Greco/Egyptian forms.

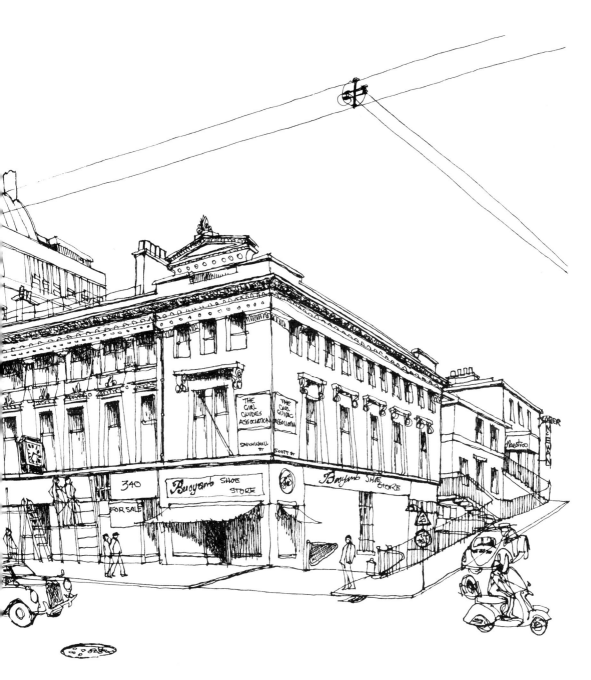

Thomson rarely worked in any other
style. He revered the pure rationale of
ancient Greek buildings, feeling
perhaps that their style lent an order
and authority to an architecturally
disturbed world.

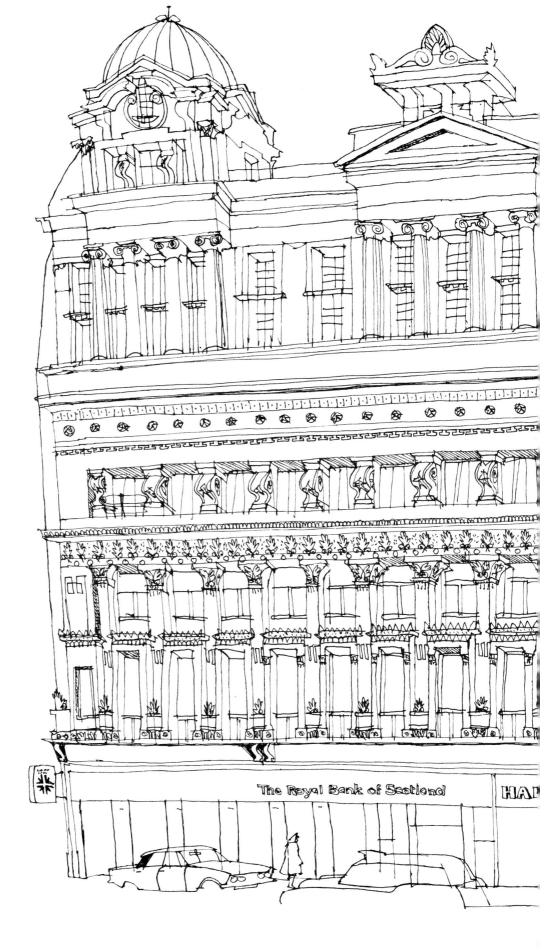

The Royal Bank of Scotland HA

40

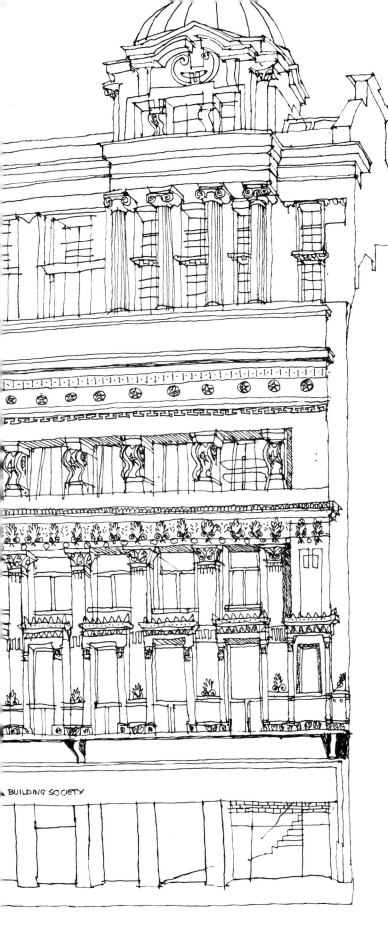

BUILDING SOCIETY

Thomson's work shuns the decorative excesses seen in other Victorian buildings (see pages 88/89 for example). A closer look however, reveals that they are often delicately engraved or carved with Greek and Egyptianesque motifs. Grosvenor Buildings (1859/61) in Gordon Street is decorated in this way, a sort of superior wallpaper you might say, although from a distance the façade looks restrained and functional.

The ungainly Baroque top part of the building is not Thomson's work. It was added in 1907 long after his death. Yet this mock-palatial pile of stone, far from spoiling the dignity of the Thomson structure below, only makes itself look pompous and silly by comparison – Beethoven assailed by Liberace.

' Greek ' Thomson could well have been called ' Egyptian ' Thomson. His buildings have as many Egyptian as Greek features. One warehouse is even called Egyptian Halls. It's in Union Street and was built in 1871/73. His Greco/Egyptianesque motifs again appear inscribed on the façade and the eaves gallery (a Thomson trademark) has a marvellous row of chubby Egyptian columns propping up a huge cornice overhang. This building really ought to be in Cairo or Luxor. Bedouin nomads should be camped outside.

Of note here, and they are wrong notes, is the concert of discord played by the unsympathetic typography on the shopfronts. Egyptian Halls is not the only building in Glasgow to be visually deafened in this way.

' Greek ' Thomson's influence in Glasgow was widespread. Many later buildings have been accredited to him but were actually designed by less talented followers. The group of warehouses (on the right middle distance) in Watson Street in the architectural melange by Glasgow Cross, were inspired by Thomson's work. Other buildings of note here are the Tolbooth Steeple (1626), the monumental Bell Street warehouse (right background) and a refurbished pub, whose rich Victorian interior boasts a huge antique Thomsonesque clock.

INDIA PALE ALE
BREWED IN SCOTLAND

N'S EXPORT

21 CLOTHING S.MEADOW LTD

CAR PARK

CORONATION RESTAURANT

Ices   Coffee   Teas   Snacks

When you've just lost the
American Civil what
you need a good stiff drink

SOUTHERN
COMFORT

TOLLCROSS

EXACT FARE - NO CHANGE GIVEN

45

1872

Lillywhites
↳ ENTRANCE 122 UNIONS →

Western Fruit Co Ltd

Clarks sho

SALE SALE GALE S

SALE

SHCE SALE SHCESALES

Warehouses may not seem architecturally promising. But the Victorians treated them as they did other buildings, lavishly decorating them in fashionable styles.

The Ca d'Oro Building (1872) built as a furniture warehouse in Union Street is a spectacular example of this. It is made almost entirely of cast-iron.

The structural use of iron and steel in Victorian times was a great technological leap forward. Although normally associated with epic structures like the Eiffel Tower and the Forth Railway Bridge, iron was commonly used in buildings, but hidden behind masonry façades.

Only a few architects realised its full potential. Cast-iron could be moulded to mass-produce arches, cornices, columns, doorways, even entire façades in complex decorative patterns. The Venetian style Ca d'Oro shows the wonderful lightness and grace which repeating patterns of cast-iron and glass could achieve. The building's only flaw is the top-heavy mansard roof (a later addition) which I have left off the page – the best place for it.

47

Cast-iron buildings were popular in America during this time. New York foundries mass-produced hundreds of Venetian style ' iron-fronts '. Many still exist there. Others were shipped west on wagon trains to be assembled piece by piece in cowboy towns on the prairies!

In Europe, Glasgow pioneered this type of building, and several fine examples still survive. The sure way to identify these is to carry a pocket magnet around – cast-iron, heavily painted over the years, can look like stone.

Gardner's furniture warehouse, the ' Iron Building ' is Glasgow's best known and finest cast-iron building. Built in Jamaica Street in 1855/56, Gardner's was designed in a subdued Venetian style by John Baird I. Architecturally it is beautifully proportioned, was structurally advanced for its time, and is of great historical importance. Its delicate iron and glass façade (which has even retained its original lettering), is maintained in immaculate condition by obviously proud owners.

INGRAM STREET

MILLAR ST

EVENING TIMES

GLASGOW HERALD

50

Glasgow's group of cast-iron buildings are unique in this country. More common in Victorian times was the jungle of intricate cast-iron ornament applied to other buildings. Ingram House for example has a forest of cast-iron on its roofline.

During the 19th century, Glasgow's foundries produced tons of cast ironwork. Walter MacFarlane's evocatively named Saracen Foundry at Possilpark even published a mail order catalogue full of cast-iron fountains, balustrades, lamp-posts, porches and doorways, many of which were shipped as ballast to the colonies. You can still find more Glasgow cast-iron in India and Australia than in the city itself.

Much of Glasgow's decorative cast-iron was melted down during the last war to make battleships (or so the propaganda said). Fortunately some pieces still remain like this Walter MacFarlane fountain whose elaborate ironwork decorates Glasgow Green.

HOUSE 207

51

The structure in the centre of the drawing is one of the most impressive surviving examples of Victorian cast ironwork in the city. This is the ' Umbrella ' at Bridgeton Cross, cast at George Smith and Company's Sun

Foundry in Parlimentary Road. Surrounded by traffic, it looks like a magic fairground roundabout and adds a touch of serendipity to an area blitzed by re-development. Also of interest is the whimsical onion-domed tenement – Moscow in Glasgow's east end.

AMUSEMENTS POOL

VIDEO GAMES

Not far from Bridgeton Cross is
' Barrowland ' – Glasgow's flea
market. There aren't many buildings
left here, except these tweedle-dum
and tweedle-dee warehouses in Bain
Street. They are not examples of

' great ' architecture, in fact they look
distinctly seedy, but with their
patterned brick-arches and unusual
oriel windows they are attractive in an
unassuming way.

Glasgow's minor industrial buildings, usually solidly built, utilitarian and red-brick, patterned in Italianate style, tend to be overlooked. Conservation seems to pass them by. Yet they are almost always attractive and ideal for conversion. The ' Barrowland ' warehouse twins and

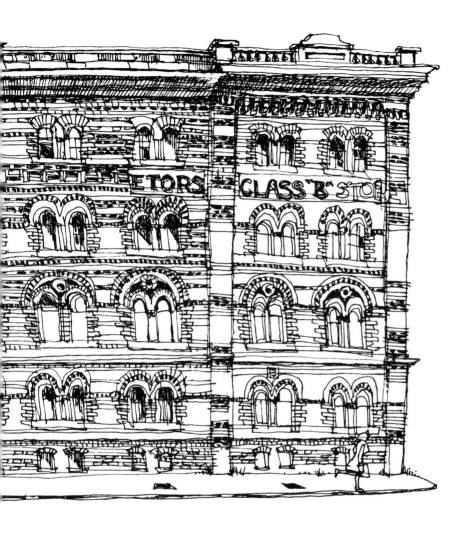

this building, Kingston Grain Mills,
are good examples.

Built in 1875, Kingston Grain Mills
had a wonderful Moorish/Byzantine
pattern of red and white brickwork.
Looking like something out of the
Arabian Nights, it shone like a jewel in
the desert of demolition all around. It
could have been polished and
restored. It was torn down in 1978.

Eagle Buildings seems to be going the
same way as Kingston Grain Mills. It
stands in sorry dilapidation in
Bothwell Street awaiting its fate...
restoration, I hope.

It is yet another Venetian style
building. Venice, with its imperial

history and maritime trade was
considered a good architectural model
by Glasgow's Victorian merchants.
They emulated the great Venetian
merchant patricians of the past and
clothed their own buildings in the
styles of the Italian city.

Eagle Buildings is an important
reminder of this colourful
cross-cultural connection. It now
stands alone, its large stone eagle
perched above the concave façade,
surveying warily the adjacent modern
blocks which encroach on its territory.

At first glance this building may look like a palace or an expensive municipal edifice. It is neither. It's a warehouse. Not an ordinary warehouse, but a Victorian one. Only the Victorians built common structures like warehouses in such a grand and extravagently ostentatious way.

This one in Morrison Street (the old SCWS headquarters) was completed in 1897 and designed in rich French Renaissance style by architects Bruce and Hay. It was rumoured at the time that they had re-used their unsuccessful City Chambers competition submission – a rumour hotly denied by the two architects. Nevertheless the SCWS building would not look out of place in George Square.

We ought to be grateful to the Victorians for their enlightened folly in designing such marvellously useless decorative façades. These extra-ordinary buildings contribute con-siderably to the rich and varied atmosphere of industrial cities like Glasgow. The SCWS building – the only building in the city to dwarf the urban motorway – enlivens what is now a rundown part of town.

CO:OPERATIVE WHOLESALE

SOCIETY·LIMITED

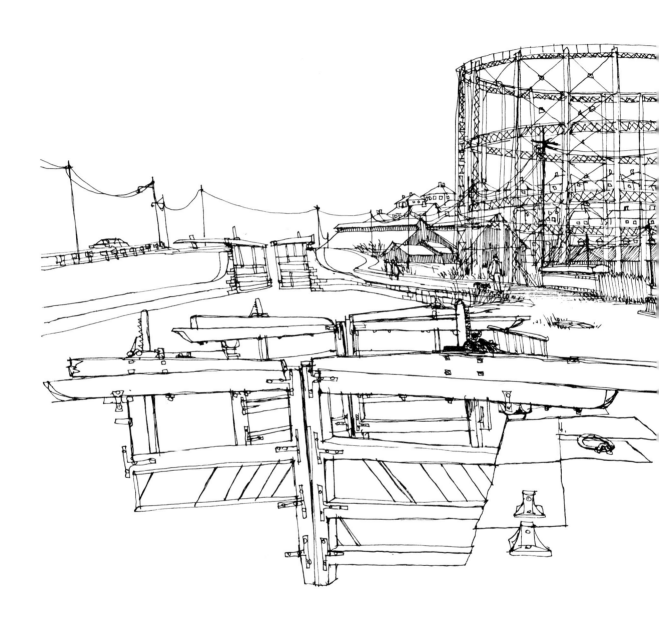

Glasgow's abandoned industrial districts can look depressing. The buildings which remain in these bleak, wasted areas look like debris on a beach to which the tide has never returned. Along the once picturesque Forth and Clyde canal, completed in 1790, superseded by Victorian railways, and closed in the 1960s, the scene is the same; rusting lock gates, overgrown towpaths, redundant factories and decaying warehouses – occasionally brightened by incongruously pretty lock-keepers' cottages. But all around is a haunting and melancholy sense of times past.

The banks of the Forth and Clyde canal were once dominated by Glasgow's most impressive example of industrial architecture. This was Pinkston Power Station at Port Dundas.

This monumental twin-chimneyed red-brick building was put up in 1900 for the electrification of the city tramway system . A building of operatic proportions, its skyscraping chimneys could be seen for miles around. It unequivocably conveyed an overpowering expression of its purpose, characteristic of the best industrial architecture of its day.

Pinkston was demolished recently, crumbling to the ground like a disintegrating dinosaur. Perhaps its time had passed, but it was distressing to see this noble building pulled down.

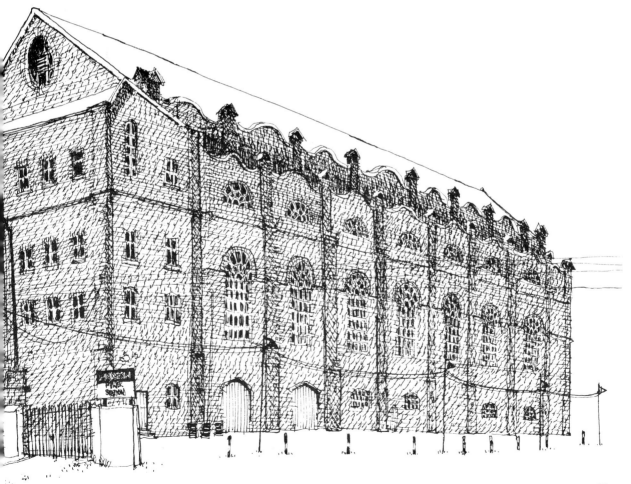

65

An equally impressive industrial monument is the Finnieston Crane. Some day, if it survives long enough, future Glaswegians will gaze on it with awe and wonder, as we scan the Pyramids of Egypt or ancient Rome. It should become a fitting reminder to Glasgow's days of imperial power and glory.

It was designed to load steam locomotives, which came down from Springburn on low-loaders, through the city streets, for export overseas. It is still used, periodically, for boilers and other heavy loads. It also is a roosting spot for Glasgow's displaced starlings which have been chased away for defacing buildings in the city centre.

To the left of the crane is the northern entrance and lift shaft of the 1905 Clyde Harbour Tunnel. A twin structure stands on the other side of the river. This tunnel, with its interior elevator shafts, down which pedestrians and vehicles plumbed mysterious Piranesian depths below the river, is an evocative Victorian relic worth keeping. It is closed at present, but it could become a useful asset in the Queen's Dock area due for re-development as an international exhibition centre. Both the tunnel and the crane may even become tourist attractions!

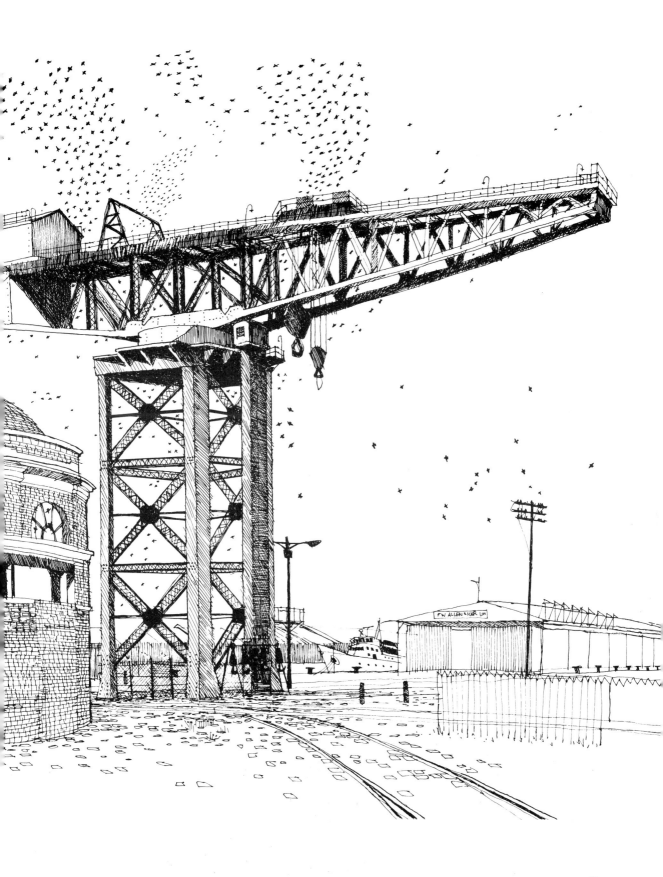

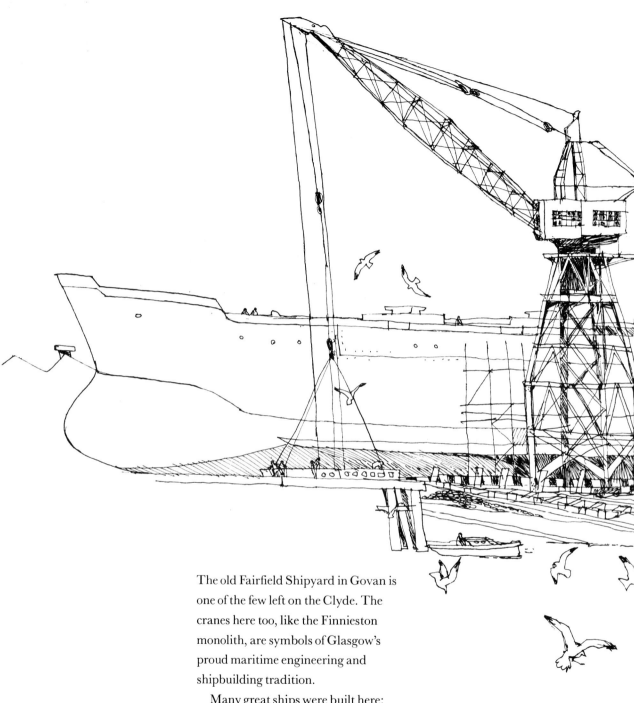

The old Fairfield Shipyard in Govan is one of the few left on the Clyde. The cranes here too, like the Finnieston monolith, are symbols of Glasgow's proud maritime engineering and shipbuilding tradition.

Many great ships were built here: the Empress liners for the Canadian Pacific, dreadnoughts for the Royal

Navy, even a yacht for the Tsar of Russia. Fewer ships are now built in Glasgow, but as today's less romantic bulk carriers slide down the Govan slipways, they carry with them a Clydebuilt tradition going back over 150 years.

Although not strictly architectural, these gaunt grey cranes and the ships built beneath them still lend the city a sense, albeit diminishing, of Victorian industrial grandeur. Glasgow's skyline and spirit would be lessened without their presence.

Many of Glasgow's Victorian
magnates had philanthropic ideals.
Whether through guilt or genuine
social conscience, they founded
libraries and parks and erected public
buildings in their name. The 1902/06
Pearce Institute at Govan Cross was
financed by a chairman of Fairfield's,

Sir William Pearce, for the benefit of the people of Govan.

Pearce himself, or rather his black statue, stands outside where he beholds his works ... and probably despairs. Govan, besieged by a barrage of redevelopment, is no longer the moderately prosperous shipyard burgh it once was. The Pearce Institute, built in attractive Scottish Renaissance style and topped with its toy sailing ship, is one of the few buildings in the area to have escaped demolition.

Yet another symbol of Glasgow's maritime past – the Clyde Trust Building on the waterfront at Broomielaw. It still houses the Clyde Port Authority, and although little remains of the port, the building retains its Victorian character. It is lavishly decorated with sculptural groups of Neptune and other trading and seaborne symbols, and was built in two stages, 1883/86 and 1905/08, to the designs of Sir J. J. Burnet.

The building was never completed – Glasgow's decline may have overtaken the port's architectural ambitions. It certainly looks lop-sided. The huge domed corner seems to have been planned as the central part of the edifice, but the right hand side is completely missing – an architectural unfinished symphony.

Glasgow's once bustling waterfront is now almost deserted. Few ships come within reach of the city centre, although the preserved paddle-steamer ' Waverley ' still chugs its way up and down stream during the summer months. The only permanent riverside resident is the ' Carrick ', built in 1864 and once the clipper ship 'City of Adelaide ' when it served the Australian wool trade. Now the RNVR club, she should become the first vessel in a Glasgow maritime museum. The city certainly deserves such a reminder of its past, but opportunities to acquire suitable old Clydebuilt steamships have been consistently passed by.

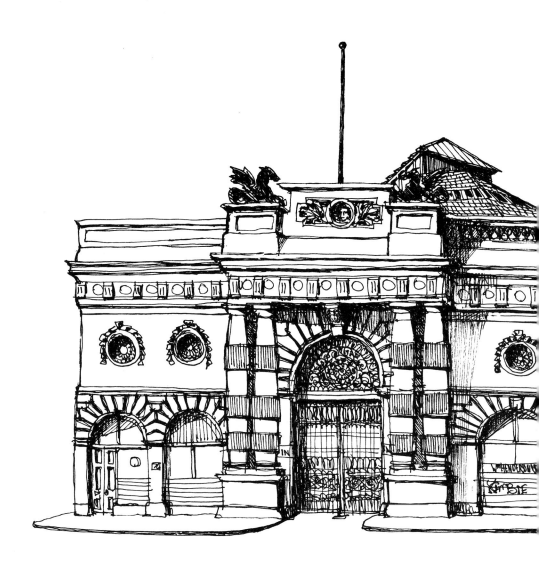

A fancy French stone façade here, concealing the cast-iron galleried interior of Glasgow's now abandoned Fish Market. Despite some decaying stonework and chipped paint, this building really does shine out. The splendidly ornate façade with its

banded columns and cast-iron gates,
all topped with a quartet of carved
seahorses is one of the most pleasingly
exuberant in the city. At present the
Fish Market is disused although
proposals exist to restore this fine
1873 riverside building.

Victorian architectural absurdity reached a peak in this building, the 1889 Templeton's Carpet Factory. You expect carpets to be richly decorated and colourful. Here the architect, William Leiper, treated the building in the same way.

Templeton's, ' as patrons of the arts, resolved . . . to erect, instead of the ordinary and common factory, something of permanent architectural interest and beauty '. It has been said that Leiper was asked what he thought was the most admirable building in the world. ' The Doge's Palace in Venice, ' he replied. Not a bad choice. So Templeton's, in the best traditions of autocratic patrons, commanded him to design them a Doge's Palace – on Glasgow Green. Which he did.

Now whether this multi-coloured brick, tile and mosaic carpet factory is beautiful or not, it is far from being common or ordinary. It is a preposterous architectural joke, an epic folly. Yet unlike more pompously designed Victorian buildings, like the SCWS warehouse, which pretend to be grand opera, Templeton's is as least genuine – genuine pantomime that is.

80

Glasgow has many Venetian style buildings. Fairfield's shipyard should have been building gondolas, not battleships. One of the best of these buildings is the exotic Venetian Gothic Stock Exchange building on Buchanan Street (1874/77). Compared to Templeton's burlesque it is much more restrained. Although both buildings use the same Venetian Gothic precedent, there is none of Templeton's vigorous pastiche here, but a more reverent and consciously architectural use of the style.

The Stock Exchange is particularly striking when morning sunlight throws dramatic shadows along the arched recesses of the façade and highlights the gabled roofline. The building was also one of the first 19th-century structures in the city to be completely rebuilt inside while retaining its original façade.

Popular Victorian architectural styles applied to prestige buildings – town halls, railway stations and churches, frequently found their way into less important buildings. These lesser structures – warehouses, banks, tenements and insurance offices, thus gained a certain contrived grandeur they otherwise would have lacked.

The Scottish baronial dressing on the two buildings shown here – one was a drapery warehouse and the other a bank branch office, shows just such a transformation. Both buildings, originally of modest purpose, are so convincingly baronial that you expect to see some laird in his tweeds pop out with a pack of gun dogs for a day on the moors.

84

It is no coincidence that many Glasgow banks and insurance companies were housed in distinguished 19th-century buildings. Many still are. Both have always sought to represent their perceived professional dignity and cultural credentials in architecture, a tradition some maintain today (Glasgow's better modern buildings are invariably prestige banks and insurance offices).

The 1904/08 Scottish Provident Institution building in St Vincent Place is typical of the grandiose style they favoured at the turn of the century. Clearly no ordinary company lives here. The building tells us so. Architecturally it is solid, dependable, with a touch of grandeur. Above all it gives an impression of confidence and stability. And what company would not wish to be portrayed as being so?

Less ponderous than the Scottish Provident building is the red sandstone Evening Citizen building, also in St Vincent Place. It was built in 1885/89 for the now defunct newspaper. It is distinguished by some subtle stonework decoration and lettering, Flemish-style gables and its unusual corner clock turret.

More immediately likeable than the Citizen building is this delightful 1896 Dutch-gabled dolls' house design in Buchanan Street. Now the Clydesdale Bank, it was originally a well known Cranston tea-room and contained Art Nouveau interiors by George Walton and Charles Rennie Mackintosh.

The façade too almost suggests Art Nouveau, though the detailing is a sort of Amsterdam Baroque. The top gable has a beautifully carved stone Glasgow coat of arms.

LIVERPOOL LONDON GLOBE

GLASGOW MARKET BLDG.   LEEDS PERMANENT BUILDING SOCIETY

88

Halfway down Hope Street is
Glasgow's most flamboyant insurance
building. It has a bewildering
complexity of columns, gables, arches,
pinnacles and statues, designed (if
indeed somebody actually did design
it – it looks put together with discarded
bits from every other building in the
city) to the praise and glory of the
Liverpool, London and Globe
Insurance Company. Who? Well
whoever they were their architectural
ambitions were certainly global. Just
about every style is here.

Remarkably, all the parts of this
Victorian architectural jumble sale fit
together in a visually satisfying way.
The building evokes wonder and
delight. Who said insurance was
boring?

The 1902 Cambridge Buildings in
Sauchiehall Street vie with the
Liverpool, London and Globe as a rich
architectural concoction. Again there
is a perplexing mixture of styles;
Greco/Egyptian, Baroque, French
Renaissance, even Jacobean in the
cupolas which sprout from the
mansard roof.

The building is the sort of gaudy
Victorian monster which modern
architectural purists used to love to
hate. Today it seems rather quaint in
its innocuous architectural fancy
dress. At least it has some humour
about it – more than can be said for the
shopping mall since built opposite.

Although taken for granted nowadays, large department stores are a fairly recent innovation. The first was the Bon Marché, built in Paris in 1876. Such was its success in selling an assortment of goods under one roof, that the idea was quickly copied across Europe and America.

Architecturally, these stores attempted to persuade their customers, through fashionable decoration and contrived atmosphere, of their prestige, modern taste and integrity. The principle holds true today. Most, whether in London, Paris, or Chicago were sumptuously embellished in palatial style.

Many have been altered, but some like the restored Fraser's in Buchanan Street survive in their original splendour. The 1885 galleried main hall, decorated in Italianate manner, with its stunning perspectives, intricate plasterwork and brass chandeliers is one of the finest of its era. A ' commercial Crystal Palace ' it was called on its opening day.

Structurally, it is also of interest. The galleries are supported on cast-iron columns hidden behind the plasterwork, while above, daylight floods in through the curved iron and glass roof. Outside, the building has a fine cast-iron façade.

Glasgow's City Chambers is a
Victorian town hall to eclipse all
others. Buildings of this type were
intended to impress. They were
manifestations of municipal pride
and prestige. Glasgow, if the City
Chambers is anything to go by, must
have had something to be proud
about. It did. It was the second city of
the British Empire, and in the 1880s it
needed a new administration building
to garland this reputation.

The building was the result of two
competitions. The eventual winner,
which stands in George Square, was
designed in Baroque/Renaissance
style by William Young, a London
Scot. It was completed in 1888 and
inaugurated by Queen Victoria
herself. The imposing façade is well
balanced, the relationship of the
central tower to the rest of the building
being particularly well handled.

Impressive as the façade is, the real
ostentation however lies inside in a
spectacular display of Victorian
opulence. There are grand stairways
of Italian marble, painted murals,
Venetian mosaics, brilliantly coloured
corridors clad in painted faience,
Spanish mahogany fittings, stained
glass, marble and alabaster columns,
and a sumptuously appointed
banqueting hall. Altogether, it is a
building of Baroque splendour, an
almost wilfully extravagant example
of Victorian civic and imperial pomp
and pride.

THERE MANELIVETH ONE FOURLANG

Like the Victorian municipal authorities, the 19th-century railway companies had architecturally exalted views of their own importance. They saw themselves as ambassadors of a new age, as dynamic and powerful as the fire-eating locomotives which hauled their trains. They matched this view in the cathedral-like stations which they built in city centres all over Europe and America.

Yet, to placate sceptical citizens, concerned over the intrusion of this new iron and steel technology into older cities, they designed their monumental station façades to look like Greek temples, Florentine palazzos,

French châteaux and Gothic cathedrals – any historical style which would confer nobility and prestige on their works.

Glasgow's Central Station hotel is typical. Built in 1884 for the Caledonian Railway, it was designed in what can best be described as Scots/Scandinavian Renaissance style – an amazing clutter of gables and windows, surmounted by a tall clock-tower from which you can tell the time from miles away. Particularly attractive is the glazed cast-iron canopy in the forecourt which still displays the Caledonian's ornamental lettering style.

Despite the money lavished on the bogus façades of these grand central stations, the true architecture of the railway age lay in the iron and glass station canopies which leap in graceful arches and girders across smoky platforms.

The interior of Glasgow's Central Station is a fine example of this marvellous architectural engineering. Steel girders are everywhere, springing out from the striking row of

octagonal steel pillars on platforms 9 and 10. On clear days with sunlight flowing in, the station takes on a beguiling, almost magical quality, with lacy patterned shadows dappling the platforms.

Also noteworthy is the huge wooden pre-1914 train indicator board. No modern electronics here, but a splendid system of manually displayed signboards, which are both efficient and legible.

Glasgow's St Enoch Station, even
more than Glasgow Central, reflected
the confident spirit of the 19th-century
railway companies. It was built for the
Glasgow and South Western Railway
in 1875/79. Its huge Gothic hotel
concealed a magnificent arched
station train shed, an engineering
spectacle of sublime grandeur. Yet
both the hotel and train shed were
demolished in the late 1970 s, victims
of planning ineptitude and political
expediency.

St Enoch's hotel did out-scale every other building in St Enoch Square. Now these other buildings can be better seen (although they are no substitute for the loss).

Among these is the scrupulously well-maintained Teacher's building and the 1896 Jacobean style St Enoch Subway Station, built to the scale of the subway trains themselves – toytown. Glasgow's subway is the only one I know where waiting passengers stand higher than the trains pulling into the stations. You feel you want to play model railways with them instead of going to work.

Smaller Victorian railway stations
also deserve attention. They were
never built to impress, unless a duke
lived nearby, in which case they
quickly sprouted ornamental turrets,
but were designed to serve small
communities and suburbs. Close to
cities, they often created their own
suburbs – developers followed the new
19th-century railway routes.

Some of the stations on the Cathcart
Circle line, like Pollokshaws East, were
originally built in open country – the
tenements and villas came later –
which explains the semi-rural
appearance of these charming
chalet-style buildings.

Glasgow's reputation for its superb Victorian architecture is growing. But demolition of buildings like the Christian Institute (shown here before its destruction in 1980) and St Enoch Station and Hotel, can do nothing but irreparably harm this reputation.

The Christian Institute was built in several stages between 1877 and 1898, by all accounts rather awkwardly. Inside, floor and window levels were in constant conflict. But from the outside it was a glorious Gothic fantasy, like something built by mad Ludwig of Bavaria. Certainly not what you'd expect to find in Glasgow. To many, it possessed no architectural merit, and was no doubt a builder's nightmare. But it did have a bizarre, ridiculous charm and it could and should have been saved.

This building was a mistake. An original Charles Rennie Mackintosh competition design was rejected and the Glasgow Art Galleries, built for the 1901 International Exhibition has ended up being the sort of hotch-potch which only the Victorians could concoct. It has been said that it was even built the wrong way round, the main entrance facing north instead of south – a fairly fundamental error.

Nevertheless this crazy mock-Renaissance art gallery seems to have aged gracefully, and it has its merits. Its eccentric arrangement of towers

and cupolas, particularly when seen at
sunset or on a misty day, are romantic,
and capture the architectural
confidence and conceit of the late
Victorian era.

Joseph Paxton's gargantuan Crystal Palace, built in London in 1850, clearly demonstrated the structural possibilities of cast-iron and glass. The decade following its construction saw many iron-framed structures built up and down the country – railway stations, iron-front warehouses like Gardner's, and conservatories. These later glass houses never matched the scale of the Crystal Palace but many were equally stylish.

One of the finest is Glasgow's

enterprising musical performances continued until 1881 when the Royal Botanic Institution bought out the lease. In 1891 the palace came under control of Glasgow Corporation.

The Kibble Palace is one of Glasgow's outstanding Victorian buildings. It is also deceptively small. As you enter the building and walk round the goldfish pond beneath a miniature dome, it is impossible to imagine the huge leafy space that awaits hidden beyond – the central circular promenade beneath the glass umbrella of the main roof.

This is where the concerts were once held, and although the concealed orchestra no longer plays, the Kibble Palace retains its magical atmosphere. You can still savour this, walking slowly round the ferns and marble statues beneath the glass roof and ornamental cast-iron columns, exchanging chilly northern days for the heat and humidity of the tropics. The nearby Palm House is equally exotic, although more a result of its trees than its architecture.

Also noteworthy is the People's Palace on Glasgow Green. Behind its sandstone façade there is a spectacular iron and glass winter garden… currently dilapidated and needing repairs.

Kibble Palace in the Botanic Gardens. It was originally built around 1860 by engineer and horticulturalist John Kibble on his estate on the shores of Loch Long, and re-erected in Glasgow in 1873 as a conservatory-cum-concert hall.

Beneath the main dome there was a huge pond, underneath which, in a watertight chamber, an orchestra could play. This ingenious arrangement allowed visitors to be serenaded among the tropical plants by invisible performers! Kibble's

Opposite the entrance to Botanic Gardens is Grosvenor Terrace. It is one of the most spectacular Victorian terraces which flank Great Western Road. It was built in 1855 in Venetian Renaissance style and looks as if it should be in St Mark's Square. The only thing missing is the Grand Canal. Yet one-third of the building is brand new.

The Grosvenor Hotel, at the east end of the terrace, was gutted by fire in 1978 leaving part of the façade damaged beyond repair. This was demolished, but it has since been faithfully re-built. Glass-reinforced concrete panels were cast in the original design and the restoration has been so studiously effected that you wouldn't know the difference.

This landmark building now looks as good as new, and much credit is due to those concerned. The rebuilding of the Grosvenor Hotel shows what can be done where enlightened concern, imagination and money are available to preserve historic buildings.

112

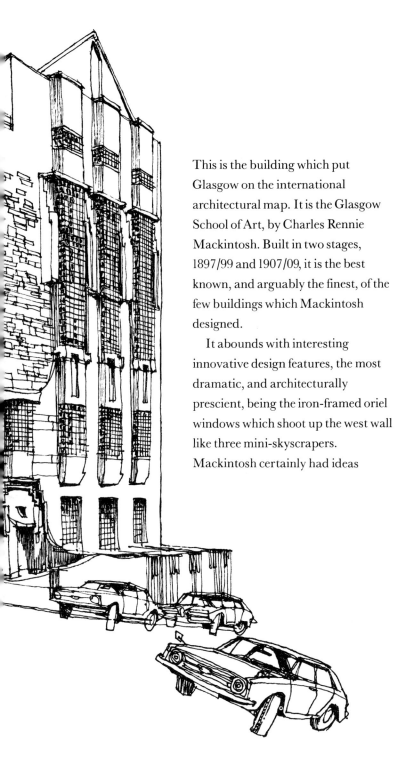

This is the building which put Glasgow on the international architectural map. It is the Glasgow School of Art, by Charles Rennie Mackintosh. Built in two stages, 1897/99 and 1907/09, it is the best known, and arguably the finest, of the few buildings which Mackintosh designed.

It abounds with interesting innovative design features, the most dramatic, and architecturally prescient, being the iron-framed oriel windows which shoot up the west wall like three mini-skyscrapers. Mackintosh certainly had ideas beyond his time. While many of his contemporaries elsewhere were building Art Gallery look-alikes, he was single-handedly dragging Victorian academic historicism, squealing, into the 20th century.

His obdurate pursuit of a new style, wrongly perceived as pure Art Nouveau – it is more geometric and peculiarly Scottish, earned him few commissions. He was undoubtedly a misfit, but by his refusal to build in the popular styles of the day he created what we now recognise as architecture of genius.

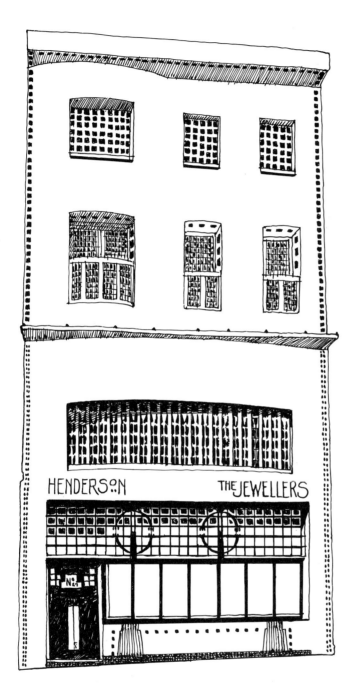

Mackintosh's contribution to European turn-of-the-century cultural life was considerable. His fame rested chiefly on interior design and painting. He not only designed avant-garde buildings, but complete interiors as well. Nor did he sit in an ivory tower. He designed a remarkable series of tea-rooms in the city for proprietor Kate Cranston. One survives, though not as a tea room, in Sauchiehall Street.

This is the Willow Tea Rooms, recently restored inside and out. The only thing missing is the Mackintosh furniture, and tea. The unusually modern (for 1904) façade really leaps out from the Victorian buildings which flank it, showing Mackintosh to have been gloriously out of step in an age of plagiarised opulence and decoration.

Mackintosh however had nothing against decoration. He simply didn't see the point of copying someone else's, so he designed his own. Yet his originality went generally un-recognised at home. But on the

continent, his work was appreciated, particularly in Vienna, where Glasgow's new architectural sparks fuelled a bigger fire – the so-called Modern Movement.

Mackintosh's pioneering modern work influenced some Glasgow architectural firms. The office of James Salmon and Son produced a number of Art Nouveau designs, including the amazing 'Hatrack' building in St. Vincent Street (1899/1902).

Known as the 'Hatrack' because of its narrow façade, it is a skilful interpretation of the Art Nouveau style. While less florid than contemporaries in Paris and Barcelona it seems, in common with most good Art Nouveau buildings, to have grown up out of the ground, rather than having been just plonked down on it. Despite its awkward site, only 10 yards wide, its minimal stonework and highly glazed façade achieves a wonderfully weightless sense of height and depth previously only possible using cast-iron.

Merchantile Chambers in Bothwell Street was also designed by the Salmon office. It was built in 1897/98. Again some Art Nouveau influence appears, hinted at rather than stated, particularly in the flowing street-level arches and the little gazebo on the top. The building also has some superfluous mock-Renaissance details – columns, heavy cornices – and one feels that these may have been a compromise by Salmon to keep the clients happy. Mackintosh of course would have had none of this. He would have walked out, which is probably why so few of his unconventional designs got built.

No book on Glasgow would be complete without some pubs. Architecturally interesting? Yes, some are. Two of the best are the Roost Bar (now the Exchequer) in Dumbarton Road and the Horseshoe Bar in Drury Street, in the city centre. The ' Roost ' has a unique and beautifully carved wooden Art Nouveau façade, fitted around 1900. It is as much a delight to the eye as a wee dram is to the taste buds inside.

The ' Horseshoe ' too, offers similar pleasures. Inside, beyond the immaculately cut lettering on its façade, it has a gloriously shabby Victorian interior of stunning opulence: huge gilt mirrors from floor to ceiling, Corinthian columns, ornamental clocks, brass candelabra, a gilt statue of a blacksmith hammering away (the site was once a stable), and as its centrepiece a magnificent horseshoe-shaped bar. It's like having a pint in the Palace of Versailles.

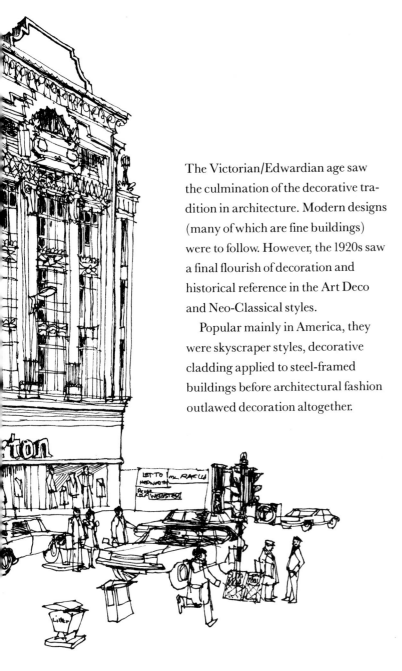

The Victorian/Edwardian age saw the culmination of the decorative tradition in architecture. Modern designs (many of which are fine buildings) were to follow. However, the 1920s saw a final flourish of decoration and historical reference in the Art Deco and Neo-Classical styles.

Popular mainly in America, they were skyscraper styles, decorative cladding applied to steel-framed buildings before architectural fashion outlawed decoration altogether.

Glasgow's Burton building at the bottom of Buchanan Street is a good example of Art Deco. It displays the bizarre characteristics of the style – Greco/Egyptian and Hollywood Aztec allied to the harsh geometry of the machine age. The result looks like a Hollywood set from Ben Hur, an allusion not out of place as many cinemas were built in the style. Not immediately likeable, the building is more extraordinary than attractive.

BANK OF SCOTLAND

BANK OF SCOTLAND
ST VINCENT STREET

BANK OF SCOT
REN
STR

Glasgow's best example of the 1920s' Neo-Classical style is the Bank of Scotland building at the corner of St Vincent and Renfield Streets, a massive structure of Ionic columns and pilasters, topped with a cornice so heavy you wouldn't think the building could support it.

This financial fortress could withstand an artillery barrage: the walls look 4 feet thick. They're not. They don't even hold the building up. Inside there is a modern steel frame. All the 'Greek' stonework is for show.

This building, and others like it, may not be Victorian. But in an age where it's difficult to tell if a school is a railway station or a town hall, it at least seems visually positive about its function. If these early 20th-century monuments survive, they, and some recent modern buildings too, will acquire the patina of time which now makes Victorian architecture so attractive.

St Vincent Street Church tower

Architecture has always moved in cycles. The Victorians reacted against Georgian severity just as 20th-century architects have in turn reviled Victorian decorative excess. Today a reaction has set in against the dogmatic architectural puritanism which modern architects, until recently, promulgated.

Every age leaves its heritage of fine buildings. Many buildings of the 20th century have lasting merit, although the visually jerry-built office blocks and failed Utopian planning schemes which litter our cities may become, for future generations, evidence of an architectural dark age.

These architectural disasters, if you look at them, represent not the cultivation of individuality and the human spirit, but its suppression. Many architects recognise this criticism. They are trying to find new, or adaptable older forms of architectural expression. Forms that people will accept, appreciate, and above all admire. They can only do this in part with some reference to the past, and it is important that we keep this past intact for them to refer to. The senseless slaughter of older buildings denies modern architecture the visual counterpoint and historical context in which it is best seen.

Robin Ward was born and educated in Glasgow. He has worked as a labourer with the Forestry Commission and as a traffic officer at Glasgow Airport. Like many Glaswegians of the past he emigrated to Canada, where he worked fur trading with Red Indians for the Hudson Bay Company in the wilds of northern Manitoba, and then as a miner, working underground.

In 1972 he returned to Scotland and studied for several years at the Glasgow School of Art, during which time he contributed a series of illustrated features commissioned by the *Glasgow Herald* on the city's architecture, much of which, to his dismay, had been demolished while he was abroad.

Robin Ward currently works as a graphic designer with the BBC.

Kingston Grain Mills – demolished 1978